Perfect Disappearance

Martha Rhodes

New Issues Poetry & Prose

A Green Rose Book
Selected by David Dodd Lee

New Issues Poetry & Prose
The College of Arts and Sciences
Western Michigan University
Kalamazoo, Michigan 49008

First Edition, 2000.

ISBN: 0-932826-99-7 (paperbound)

Library of Congress Cataloging-in-Publication Data:
Rhodes, Martha
Perfect Disappearance/Martha Rhodes
Library of Congress Catalog Card Number (99-85952)

Art Direction: Tricia Hennessy
Design: Jeff Pansé
Production: Paul Sizer
                   The Design Center, Department of Art
                   College of Fine Arts
                   Western Michigan University
Printing: Courier Corporation

Perfect Disappearance

Martha Rhodes

New Issues

WESTERN MICHIGAN UNIVERSITY

Perfect Disappearance

Also by Martha Rhodes

At the Gate

for Jean Alain Brunel

and for Laure-Anne Bosselaar
and Katherine Titus

Contents

*Whanne thou wenest for to
slepe, so fulle of peyne
shalt thou crepe.*
        —anonymous

One

Into the Lake, the House

The wind's having trouble
deciding whether
to raise the house
or not,
ripping it across the sky, or
ever so gently brushing by,
barely a shudder.

Unlike some,
less cautious, less
concerned, this wind
is tired of tragedies—
acres of strewn possessions
(vases, shoes)—
and may prefer to be benevolent,
the kind of wind people invite
to luncheon in July, families
whispering to wilting walls, *oh*
for a bit of wind
to stir up the air
so we can breathe . . .

On days like this, even kids
close shop—abandoned lemonade stands
haunt the common, across from the one-room museum,
its permanent display of arrows and beads.

I feel so heavy,
sighs one pregnant woman.
I wish I could float
from here to Lake Armington—
freezing, glacier, glorious lake . . .

just two towns away, almost to Pike,
at the foot of Mount Piermont—
easy enough for the wind to plunk
the black-shuttered white house
and all its contents into the water:
matching armoires bought in Henniker,
the upright piano, the husband

with his pregnant wife—
the lake would barely swell.

Over the Presidentials,
the wind is gaining strength.
It's making up its mind.

Pattern of Cracks

The plasterer, most assuredly,
hasn't been here (he'd leave his pail
or trowel behind), besides
I haven't left the room all day—
too strange outside:

a 1946 piper-yellow Piper Cub
about to land in my yard
ascends suddenly;
and the orchards cling to their dying leaves
sensing something below's more treacherous
than wind or cold . . .

Difficult to account for the ceiling,
this morning's zig-zagged pattern of cracks
now seamless, no thanks to me,
a step ladder's third rung higher
than I've ever chanced. Impossible
impossible, such fine, expertly
crafted work, faultless as it dries
above me, shrinks and cures.

Around, My Shadow

Your arm around the space
Where my back was—asleep, you
Kiss air, stroke air and sheets

I am circling myself
Four hundred miles around, my shadow
The time it takes

Large enough
Invisible
At last

Always when I was under you
On top of you, my mouth
Was always full, my stomach, not

Last night I plucked whole cows
From clouds, this morning
Elephants as appetizers, herds

The lake rises when I wade,
One sip its bed is dry—here, for you
The last of the lake in a cup

Cat

I yelled at her
Picked her up, shook her
Threw her down
And she jumped up again
To get at the roast chicken
She was purring and squawking as usual

Purring and eating chicken
Her tiger tail pointing to heaven
I couldn't stand that she was dying
And had taken it out on her
She looked so cheerful, dying
Chirping as always

We brought her again to the clinic
I visited the next day
And signed the paper
While she sniffed my ear and sighed
Then draped herself down my back
Front claws kneading

It would take me (*nine* months
I realize now) nine months
To get another

Disguised

Bark-stripped and leafless

They're roped up in my cellar
All are young, all are male

I've taken them from parks
Neighbors' lawns and sidewalks
Little saplings, unprotected

Except sometimes iron grates
Sheltering their roots; I take them
At night, occasionally by day
Disguised as a city worker

Their limbs, their small
Round trunks so precisely
Snapped apart, oh
My sweet syrup'd darlings
Whom no one will look for

This One Especially

Who was I following all day ending up
at the piers, dangerous and loose-planked?

Last night, my sister telling me,
"We have a brother somewhere"—

in this world a brother older
than the marriage that bore us.

And today, this one especially,
of all the many men I've watched

the most likely, so abandoned, not
ever brought riding with sisters

through the out-back preservation buffered by swamp,
so abandoned, not growing up in our ranch house—

where has he been, not protecting me,
always left behind,

poor brother whom I never kissed before,
what was he doing out there by himself,

mid-day, not working (like me),
needing also a haircut,

but clean,
I was happy to see that about him.

How Fast

Can you tell me where my car is,
please
and then, when I'm in it, where
to put it, which way (and how long) to turn it
from exactly where it is
and then what, what, once turned?

Can you tell me where my car is?

And my keys, how to turn *them*,
how to place my foot
on which pedal, and my hands
can you put your hands where mine should go?

Can you tell me if I am always like this,

when I am sleeping, do I know on my own
when to turn over, which way to lay my body across the bed,
which way to place my head and arms, how far
to pull the blanket up, how to rise
in the middle of the night when my body needs,
and where to walk, from bed to where? Do I call for you
even then? I'm asking you,

in this lot, near my parents' house,
how do I get to that house, theirs
the only one on the street I can't see, so clouded
it is with smoke. Which way to that fire,
please,
how to reach that fire, please, and then
how do I rotate my body, and how fast,
if I reach there, where
will I find the pit, the stake

Our father at 80 has moved to the country where

he's no longer poisoned
every Sabbath dinner by imagined sons
owing him money (his one real son
birthed into a receptacle somewhere &
all this revealed one night
when our father was far past drunk
transported elsewhere, shameful
untraceable, not-of-our-mother boychik,
our brother).
Our father, splitting up wood,
dips his cut finger
into a canteen of bourbon

recalling to us his pal Sharkey's cure
for their frequent bouts of clap
(soak the damn thing in scotch)
and recalls Sharkey hobbling down grandpa's
pawn shop aisles, futzing with watches,
pocketing rings, father in too much pain
to chase him. And always,
by the seventh day of treatment
they were running with the girls again.
My sisters and I won't stay for dinner,
(squirrels steeping in wine).

The Party

Outside the house, behind barrels,
bikes, broken parts:
a shed.

She's never worn this kind of dress:
black silk, pink roses,
loosely laced down her back,
easily lifted above her hips,
a slow tug over her breasts;
he stops her there.
Now she's breathing
through the dark skirt,
and watching him.

This man knows what she's just now
learning—that for her
it's best this way—
leaning back, her legs hugging
a stranger's waist.

Finished now and outside the shed,
the man sees a friend slumped in a wheelchair,
kiss him, darlin' kiss my buddy,
kiss him where he'll feel it (anywhere chest-up),
and back in the shed, she does, both men,
while the party's spreading onto neighbors' yards.

Years from now, when she marries,
as she lifts the hem of her gown
exposing the ruffled garter she'll twirl
above her head, she'll remember two men,
those strangers in a broken shack,
rotting and sinking, pegboards and nails—
and dancing, dancing and music
and Japanese lanterns
yards away.

In bed, in this

New England inn
I'm 40 like I am, but
tinseled
slippery
straddling tables
dipping my toes
into men's and women's gins
vodkas
every drink
clear and iceless

I'm screwing all
the Christmas guests
the cook
the maid
her husband in his reindeer suit
and why the hell not the whole town
what's keeping *you* outside in the cold
I shout through the window
to the gas pumper across the street
thumbs in his pockets

In this bed when I stuff a pillow
under my nightgown I'm twenty-eight
and pregnant and reach for a towel
draped over the Windsor rocker
and bite down hard against the pain

As They Had Died

From the rim of a Mayan pit
I looked for remains of the sacrificed,
wanting to see them as they had died,
half strangled and stabbed, left
to claw for the top of the stack.

And their screeching's what
aroused me—their necks,
smooth as mine, aroused me—
young girls, even babies,
barely tooth'd, each daughter
asleep between parents,
sweetly asleep, only
seconds away from her father
discovering how wonderfully,
how easily, he might pull his girl
from her mother's folds;

it's *just* at that moment my armies
arrive, house by house,
thrusting the girls,
fresh from their mamas,
into my carts,
centuries of girls,
naked and golden.

One day she will fall

in the driveway, bedroom, shower—
break her pelvic bone, miss the toilet,
smile that her husband must clean her
and every minute stay with her—
all the necklaces and bracelets given
over years, the safe box full, elbow-deep—
        but for now, she paces the child's room
then the terrace overlooking
the husband who gardens
even at night, kneeling
in the lantern light
murdering weeds—
how capable he is

A Thorn, a Beam

(for my husband)

A twelve-inch thorn
embedded in your thigh,
or blood spurting from your ear,
a ceiling beam splitting your spine:
I'd have pried, drained, welded
  and you would have recovered.
But now, twenty years later
and not even sure why,
I've left you all week alone
with your fever: water, lemon,
a teaspoon stuck to the dresser.

Husbands

Who are these men?

They say I hired them, owe them wages.
They know the delicate handling of trees:

One describes himself and his friends
At my snake-clogged well lowering buckets—

Inside this house, chocolate and winter stir.
I refuse to remember family I had.

Off to the village: medicines,
Drinkable water, and the grocer

Who sells such items proposes
To cut my hair, repair my house.

He knows just where the bedroom paper peels—
Three ragged violets at the southeast corner—

How often he must have slept there—but with whom?
I've lived in that house alone, and always.

Destined

Though it's eight years since your death
I wait for the night you phoned me
while your baby lay blind in your arms,
her brain flooded, that sac
at the nape of her neck,
and you begging me
to end her life

who would die two days later,
drowned in her own fluids,
or had she?
You silent thereafter,
had she
how did she
did you?

And when you sank in the pond
a decade later, your children
as witnesses, I envisioned
the lilies and baby
sucking you down while I,
at surface, let you go. Yes,
I am waiting to tell you
I should have done it for you,
I could have done it, Lucy
and I would now.

Oh, Luminous

Yesterday, another dog collapsed, this one
endlessly carrying slippers and bones.

If I don't leave here now, I'll die here,
the ascent to town less than one hour

and my car headed Away, but stalled,
surrounding temperature so extreme

my skin can't distinguish
winter, summer.

In just one hour:
carrots for sight, beets for blood, oh town

where all things good. This house,
where all things bad, barren

skeleton, shelter of leaking rooms,
whose property is this property?

The owner is lost. The house has lost
the owner, the owner has lost the house.

Where there are no chairs
there are plates and silver

scattered across the lawn—sunless,
seedless, wormless lawn—

even the dead and the ones
underneath the dead

crawl away, away, deeper down,
do I still have time?

Oh luminous town.

Two

Child and Swamp

A cautious child
does not, on Thursday,
point at him
a venomous pencil
and on Friday see
a black tributary
current deliberately
up his arm. A cautious
child does not swim,
all summer, in a hidden
creek, her braids
fanning bottom, her
mouth refusing air
minutes more each day.
A cautious child
does not lie naked
and cold in the wet
nor breathe in mud
vapors, nor eat mud
nor let creatures
pass their diseases
through her skin.
A cautious child
jumps into green/
black water only
if startled or fooled
when she believes
she must, for her life,
kick face-down faster
than she can.

It being forbidden

to excuse oneself from table
before each morsel is chewed and swallowed;
it being forbidden to laugh
unless he conducts, pitch and duration,
his arms raised, our sisterly heads shamed
downward; it being forbidden
to invite another to that table who dares
to be more handsome and charming than he.

It being commanded to worship
that occupier of the armed-chair,
carver of pheasants, rabbinic imposter,
tweed-suited weekend gardener,
peddler of diamonds to the ghetto

and we do worship him
for plentiful is his table,
joyous the summer camps,
vast the Canadian forests,
the Caribbean Sea.

He who orchestrates with knife and fork
pulls us to our knees
and we pray with him who whispers
do you love me
and we cry with him who whimpers
no one loves me
and we kiss him on his temple
no one touches me
and we remain in his house
longer than we ought, for he prophesies
even you shall leave me
and when we do leave him, as we must,
we transplant lilacs and peonies from his garden
to ours so that he shall bloom
beneath our windows.

Why They Cannot Move

Now he stands
A big man
Taller than oaks
In the yard
A daughter squeaks
In his shoes

Wife unties apron
Exposing
In the yard
Turning and grilling
Skewers of panties
He's collected

Now he sleeps
Unable to grab, to chase
Through the yard. He cannot
Turn over, he cannot move
Why he cannot cry for help
Men and women

Chase him through kitchens
Jack knives, butcher,
Pen knives stick him
Little man
Pink with fat welts and helpless
Children poking holes in him

Why he is helpless now
While he sleeps he flutters
Smaller than a child
In the alley
Smaller than the baby
On Mount Washington

His mother dangled naked
Smaller than the son
Smaller than the daughter
Than the wife

The man
Whom his own daughter
Dreams of as taller
Than the oak in her yard
That man's arms and legs
Longer than willow branches
Why can't she turn herself over
Why can't she move while she sleeps

Without Gloves

My sister and I are fighting as always
in dreams, our faces an inch apart.
On the counter: carving knives and platters
(perhaps Mother's)
(perhaps Mother's dead in the cabinet)

What should we do?
Don't pick up the knives.
Don't touch them without gloves.

"I hate your husband," she tells me.
"He hates you," I answer.
"He stares at my breasts."
"Wear a blouse," I tell her.

She tries to touch me as always
in dreams, I call a dog,
the biggest on the block
but a rat answers my whistle,
and attaches to my wrist.

Always rats in dreams with us
or other little rodents.
Little punctures, little nibbles,
my gnawed off little hand
and I'm unable to save it.

This Is My Mother

This is my mother,
shrunken in my hands—
an egg, translucent,
thin-membrane'd

I am clumsy with what's small
(she never let me handle
her mother's heirloom crystal)
yet now, from bed to chair—

I dare myself to drop her

A Room Where a Child

I am praying
Dreaming of a room
Where a child may rest
Unafraid of who will enter
I enter
And a child stands in her crib
For me to lift her, her hands
Lovely hands ferocious in my hair
Until I shake her hard, wanting her to cry
She cries
And I shush her
Shush

I am dreaming of a child
Who will not rest
I will not let her rest
Who bangs her head
Against my chest
Who bruises me
And will not be calmed
By a kiss or slap—all I know
To do—in my dream
I am praying for a room
Where a child may rest
Unafraid of who will enter
I will not enter, the child
Will allow me to rest, the child
Will sleep through my dream

Without Her, I

Her perfect disappearance
confuses me.
If she will not be found,
will I?

$$\frac{34}{35}$$

Three

For My Husband

The Japanese maple
Our house leaning into the next
The photo of you on this wall
Rake over shoulder
Your back to apple trees and pond
And me taking the picture
As you walked away

How much longer
Can you last without water
Fig trees sparse

The desert you walked to without me
Leaving me this swollen field, half creek
The plague, the sun, everything
So ripe

Is Still, Is Calm

Even while I'm fluffing up pillows
a sheet smoothed by my hands
is then clenched in my hands;
a cup set to dry, scattered
across the counter; sometimes
a wisp of hair, sometimes
my cat is suspect (his tail
transformed to whatever's
suddenly climbing my leg)
and my wrist pulse and temple pulse
quicken, and a blush spreads
randomly across my chest—

When at night moths follow me
from hammock
to kitchen, ignoring
the ceiling bulb,
nesting in my hair,
spawning, in seconds,
hundreds of leathery wings
my bed, my island
of flannel and lace,
is a strangler's
hand-reach away—

And in my garden the delicate
wind chime might clang wildly
though I see the magnolia branch
from which it hangs
is still, is calm.

Individuals

It was the time when birds
ceased migrating

when cats (dogs would follow shortly)
lay on bridges
highways
tracks
at night, in fog

It was the future
and adults realized
their parents had long since
died, though expected
not to

No longer did anyone have
nor desire
a family
and individuals killed only
themselves; many learned from birds
and other drunkards to swallow
beakers of fermented berries
before diving down wells—others
needed no such preparation—

it was the time
it was the future
and even the frailest
most timid
securely, and without hesitations,
walked about any hour
for no one stalked them street corner
to corner, nor worried if they chose
not, one particular night
or ever, to return home

and at every town's farmer's market
all the shovels, urns, bricks and ropes—
stacked against trucks and given away

This Cottage, This Dream

A disturbing quiet
and always this dream
whenever she's still . . .

Tar-painted skylights,
crawling cork walls
crawling
a delivery boy . . .

She must leave this place.

Men in the field waving.
They think she drives away,
for provisions, they think.
Left by her door: their gifts
of corn and tomatoes,
freshly killed chicken.

How strong the stink
from within, how loud
flies feasting till one day
mid-week one neighbor or two
enter and discover the girl
isn't dead inside,
just gone.

Having moved to a room below which
a diner, it's here she dreams
she's gently carried,
driven back . . .
(and this is what she came here for,
here, in this room, such undisturbed
sleep) . . . *men in the field,*
their pre-dawn gifts
on her porch . . .

Landmarks

1.
The Mountain

Since the morning it erupted
from my tulip beds,
uprooted the magnolia, nearly
cut me off from light,
(when I dare look up)
I measure the descent
of boulders, lava, new rivers.
I've limited my movements.
One heavy step might
heave the mountain higher.

2.
Others

Now, by me
a grandmother mist
hovers, and generations
of generations stack themselves
against these walls, familiar
imaginings tracking me
to this tiniest corner
where I was sure
I'd disappeared.

3.
Tropic

No one dresses
in this hovel.
We grow bodiless,
almost merely shadows.
At night, most
weep freely, recalling
bellies, thighs—

4.
Plot

Sisters, uncles, nieces, fathers,
All pressed into this
Small earth
She's swallowing his chest, his hand's
In her thigh, thin sheets
Our grandmothers wove
Pine boxes our grandfathers carved
Crumbling
Small continents rubbing & rubbing
When will their limbs
Cease reaching, by when must I say, Yes
Put me down here

5.
New Lands

Here lands rise
through lost, imagined
skies. Bats nose
their way past;
all of us scanning
these infant ravines.

6.
The Beach

lacquer black sand
black ocean
juxtaposed constellations
white strips painted long &
wide enough for landing

7.
Race Point

I can tell how close the tide will creep.
Loneliness doesn't matter on this dune

nor children's shrieks
over starfish and pails.

Nor does it matter who joins me.

I have one blanket, towel, and lunch.
I welcome no one, turn no one away.

Here, Entering

The ledger specifies
she died: "*April 22nd,*
her birthday, coincidentally,
yesterday."
As she turns the pages
(how does she know
turn/page . . .)
she's interested but removed:
She has no memory of crashing
any object (*car/wall*)
as if it were a hated face,
nor of husbands (*evidently three*).
No memory of the yellow cottage
pictured on this page,
of a loom, a terrace, shawls
over chairs. No memory
of dying, only her first
moment here, entering
this room. She was neither
breathing nor suffocating,
speaking nor silent,
aware, unaware of this
crowdedness, this emptiness.

Elegy

My body given away, parts
flown to other parts—a child
receives my eyes, another
my heart, the diseased organs
remain, benign now.
In death I am waiting
for my soul to arrive
that I may divide it equally
among frightened neighbors.
In death I pursue a man
younger than my father
ever was in my life.
In death I am a mother
who disowns her children
in a market parking lot.
In death a ghost lies
under me, pregnant. In death
I unbury myself and try
to extract my soul surgically;
it will not release, will not;
I discover there is no one else
this soul wishes to be.

Two Ghosts

To the woman I said,
"Margaret, you're looking well. Better than ever."

Her eyes were Pennsylvania field green
and her mouth was no longer caked white,
as when she was alive, a heavily drugged
librarian, drooling and stiff-armed.

To the man I said, "You, too, look well.
Haven't we met before?
Was it you I blind dated
at the kosher deli on 2nd Ave?
Aren't you, weren't you, Avram's older brother?
Didn't I read that you . . . "

The two side-stepped toward and around me.
They encouraged me to touch them, shake
their hands, one hand at a time.
Their skin wasn't cold, wasn't clammy.

Neither could talk to me aloud
but they did encourage me
to listen in on their thoughts, both
thinking at once, _She's_ not looking well.

So ashamed, I looked down.

She's so ashamed, I heard them think.

And then, thinking extraordinarily loudly,

Let's take her with us!

Flying from the same bridge,
at the same time, us from the high level,

she from the low, the three of us bare-foot,
our socks neatly rolled into our shoes.

We'll meet under water! Under water!
We'll hold hands, swallowing water!
Swallowing air!

Through Clouds, Their Whispers

A bridge, fallen. And so
they call me. *Lie across our river*, they beg
up through clouds, their whispers reach me.
Why should I bother? Why listen?
I have never been touched before, why now,
such intimacies—they explain how they'll
move on me, rolling, stamping.
They'll dump garbage, furniture, their murdered.
Some god-help-them will jump from me, *let them*, I'm told.

How do they want me?
On my back looking up their skirts,
staring at their bulging zippers,
into their baby carriages? Or turned over?
Never before touched,
how many hands positioning me?
Then the planting of trees up my spine as I span their ankle-deep river.
They will celebrate me with bandstands, dog runs, bike paths.
I have never been, nor have I, touched. Do I dare do this?

When they walk across who will first wrap her long legs around me,
roll down that hill into this river, lie on its banks, spreading wide
so the breeze of me may dry her every and all afternoon, she will
walk across the small of my back, she will lie on my back,
gently day and night I will swing her to sleep.

But if my arms tire, and my legs
and my ribs, when they begin to crack
and I can no longer reach shore-to-shore (yes
even *our* bones shrink), which of you cousins
will listen if I call upward,
will any of you come for me,
or even remember me,
how twice each day
I stand in your midst—

we scrub and groom ourselves
with so much hope, as if
at last, in these clouds,
someone's there for each of us,
for each, a kiss.

Acknowledgments

Thanks to the editors of the following magazines in which these poems have originally appeared, some in different versions.

Agni: "Elegy," "How Fast"

American Poetry Review: "As They Had Died,"
   "Our father at 80 has moved to the country where,"
   "For My Husband"

The Boston Phoenix: "This One Especially"

Columbia: "Destined," "Disguised," "Two Ghosts"

Gulf Coast: "The Party"

Harvard Review: "This Cottage, This Dream"

The Isle Review: "Pattern of Cracks," "Cat"

Many Mountains Moving: "Through Clouds, Their Whispers"

Marlboro Review: "A Room Where a Child,"
   "Into the Lake, the House"

Ploughshares: "Oh, Luminous," "Without Gloves"

Provincetown Arts: "Individuals"

Salamander: "It being forbidden"

Third Coast: "Child and Swamp," "Why They Cannot Move"

Night Out: "In bed, in this" (Milkweed Editions, 1997,
   Kurt Brown and Laure-Anne Bosselaar, editors)

Thank you to The MacDowell Colony and The Millay Colony for the Arts for offering me residency fellowships. Thank you to the following writers: Joan Aleshire and Ellen Bryant Voigt for their in depth responses to the manuscript; Ruth Anderson Barnett, Sarah Blake, Doreen Gildroy, Pat Mangan, D. Nurkse, Dzvinia Orlowsky, Marcia Pelletiere, Frazier Russell, Michael Ryan, and Gail Segal for ongoing support and encouragement. And thanks to Ellen Dudley for the example of her own fierce and wonderful poems.

"Cat" is dedicated to Laure-Anne Bosselaar; "For My Husband" is dedicated to Jean Alain Brunel; "Pattern of Cracks" is dedicated to SM Clark and Peter Josyph; "Two Ghosts" is dedicated to D. Nurkse.

photo by Peggy Eliot

Martha Rhodes is the author of *At the Gate* (Provincetown Arts Press, 1995) and the Director and one of the Founding Editors of Four Way Books, an independent literary press. She is also the Executive Founding Director of The CCS Reading Series. She teaches writing at New School University and in the MFA Program at Emerson College. She lives in New York City.

New Issues Poetry & Prose

Editor, Herbert Scott

James Armstrong, *Monument in a Summer Hat*
Anthony Butts, *Fifth Season*
Gladys Cardiff, *A Bare Unpainted Table*
Lisa Fishman, *The Deep Heart's Core Is a Suitcase*
Joseph Featherstone, *Brace's Cove*
Robert Grunst, *The Smallest Bird in North America*
Edward Haworth Hoeppner, *Rain Through High Windows*
Josie Kearns, *New Numbers*
Lance Larsen, *Erasable Walls*
David Dodd Lee, *Downsides of Fish Culture*
Deanne Lundin, *The Ginseng Hunter's Notebook*
Joy Manesiotis, *They Sing to Her Bones*
David Marlatt, *A Hog Slaughtering Woman*
Paula McLain, *Less of Her*
Malena Mörling, *Ocean Avenue*
Julie Moulds, *The Woman With a Cubed Head*
Marsha de la O, *Black Hope*
C. Mikal Oness, *Water Becomes Bone*
Margaret Rabb, *Granite Dives*
Rebecca Reynolds, *Daughter of the Hangnail*
Martha Rhodes, *Perfect Disappearance*
John Rybicki, *Traveling at High Speeds*
Mark Scott, *Tactile Values*
Diane Seuss-Brakeman, *It Blows You Hollow*
Marc Sheehan, *Greatest Hits*
Phillip Sterling, *Mutual Shores*
Angela Sorby, *Distance Learning*
Russell Thorburn, *Approximate Desire*
Robert Vandermolen, *Breath*
Martin Walls, *Small Human Detail in Care of National Trust*
Patricia Jabbeh Wesley, *Before the Palm Could Bloom:*
    Poems of Africa